Social Problems: A 1965 Research Paper

I0789528

by

Bob Ferguson

Copyright © October, 2020 Bob
Ferguson
All rights reserved.
ISBN: 9798693836457

Prologue

With the Pandemic in full swing I was sifting through vintage clothes, photographs, and old papers and I ran across the best term paper I ever wrote. It contains my beliefs about poverty, police, juvenile delinquency, education, and what was termed backed then as the "Negro Problem." All are revered and deserve a spot on a shelf somewhere. It's the sort of thing I do every 30 years or so. It's a trip down memory lane, which is getting shorter. My kids will have to throw it out, I simply can't throw out 50-yearold baby shoes.

My views contained in this work from 1965 are the same opinions I espouse today and about the same problems we are facing in 2020. And get this, my ideas are beginning to be implemented as I write this tome. This digest is written for the do-good folks who rail against systemic racism, embrace women's rights, endorse the LGBTQRSTUwhatever, but feel perfectly entitled to call me an "Old, Privileged, White, Guy" without recognizing the racism, agism, and gender bias in their own statement. BTW, I am also FAT so please make it a proper insult.

Every page of the term paper is copied as exact as I can make it, warts, and all. I have added no more than a word or two for clarity. The original has the foibles of being written on E-Z Erase paper, on an ancient portable Royal typewriter that makes some letters barely readable. In the late 60's my brother, Larry frequently used it for a few of his papers and received A's and B's on most of them. It got some mileage, so I am resurrecting it at this time as proof positive that I have done my share to promote awareness about the problems causing the Portland riots. I am a devout capitalist who believes in social programs that will do the most good for the most people. You will find more information in a few of my other books:

Some Days Chicken, Some Days Feathers
The Colossal Life of Mr. Average
Shut Up and Take Notes: It's my turn to talk about Vietnam
It's Time to Write Your Memoir! A Guide to Getting Your Story Published for The Price of a Latte!

Social Problems

by
Bob Ferguson

Social Problems
11:20
Professor Johnson

<u>Social</u> <u>Problems</u>

The books that we have read and discussed in class have
produced quite a change in my outlook on sociology and life
in general. I was aware there were serious social problems
in our society, but as to the extent of those problems I was
really unaware. As most other people on a small campus, I
limited my vision to those social problems which concerned
only myself. When I read about the problems such as poverty, the
Negro problem, juvenile delinquency, drug addictions, the corrupt-
tion in business and etc., I felt that all the sociologists
needed to solve these problems was more money an better programs.
This course and the books we have read and discussed have
broadened this telescopic view.

The purpose of this paper is to try to express my understanding of society and it's problems as I now understand them.
This, I feel, can best be done by: (1) Carefully considering
What each author has said about the particular problems they
have discussed, (2) Try to present the problems as I
see them in their relation to society, rather than each as a
separate entity of society, (3) Finally, I am going to express my own opinions and experiences regarding the problems as
much as I am able to with my limited knowledge of these many
faceted problems.

Since this is a somewhat of an experimental type of class, I am going to write an experimental type of paper. Almost all of the papers a college student writes are of the type where he is given a topic to write upon. The student then is to research the details of the topic and then record them in a research paper. From this, the student is expected to know the facts of the case, so to speak. Social problems deal with human interaction, and I don't feel we can do the topic justice with this type of paper. This paper is going to be different in the sense that I have attempted to understand the material and apply it to my own philosophy of the social sciences and also apply the information to my own social values.

Social problems are phenomena that are generally considered to be undesirable and are, in large part, dependent upon our social structure. Any fundamental change in these phenomena is dependent upon a fundamental change in the social structure. If we attempt to change or eliminate a problem, we must prepare ourselves to face a different kind of problem. Every form of organization, short of absolute perfection, must pay the price of some type of social problem. According to our values, we may eliminate one type of problem, but this problem will be replaced with another. Our values will determine which of the problems we will be willing to accept. The policies that an organization makes are a result of these social values. The policies enacted verify the fact that we must pay a price for those policies.

Poverty is the price we are paying for several of our social values. According to Michael Harrington's book, The Other America, between 40,000,000 and 50,000,000 people are living in a state of poverty (5, p., 173). To most of us these are staggering figures, but he seems to have well-documented his statistics. Most of us, in the traditional middle-class viewpoint, say, "Why don't these people help themselves?" Little do we realize the true problems of the poor. There are many reasons why people are poor, and we are surprised to find out that the generous public actually exploits the poor and makes their conditions worse.

Technological advancement is the cry of those who are ~~not~~ living in poverty. While society advances there are those who will become immune to progress. Those people with mental or physical disabilities who will be replaced by automation will not advance. There is no more need for the unskilled or semi-skilled laborer, and for most of those laid off due to automation it can mean a one-way trip to poverty. Others that are affected by technological advances are the small farmers who find that they can no longer compete with the larger, mechanized farms. The Negroes are the first to be fired and the last to be hired where automation strikes. The old people who are no longer able to get employment of any type are hurt because of the rise of the cost-of-living that automation brings, while yet their income remains the same.

Once these people become poor thy are caught up in a vicious cycle of poverty. Poverty brings a new way of life to them. They develop a language of the poor, a psychology   of the poor, and a world view of the poor. They develop a relatively distinct, but not a totally separate part of society. Thus, poverty becomes a subculture. Those who are born into this culture tends to perpetuate its own existence. The young adopt those values and attitudes of the culture. Their values, which would be considered deviate behavior in our society, are the accepted pattern of behavior in their culture.

These people do not become poor by their own choice. Unless they were born into the culture, they once had skills which provided them with a living. These skills are no longer as valuable as they once were. The men are forced to take jobs in kitchens and sweat shops working for a small fraction of their original wages. The management, who are often the most respected people in town, are exploiting the situation of the poor by paying them .68 cents an hour. [My "Shut Up" book exposes Nike's decades of exploitation of the Vietnamese workers in their Vietnam factories.]

The men become despondent when they find that the automation that displaced them from one job follows them into other fields. Such is the case of the displaced coal miner who was displaced by machines in the mines. He then turned to the steel industry for work, where he was displaced again.

It appears on the surface that these people could solve their plight by moving. However, the person who only has a few more years to work for the company before he receives his pension cannot afford to leave, so he stays hoping that some- thing will come up so he can receive his pension. The most important reason that people cannot move is the fact that they are tied down by home ownership. Others have deeply planted roots in the community that would make it impossible to leave. Another important reason that they do not move is because the unskilled laborer would have a difficult time getting employment anywhere (5, p., 38). The young adventurous type could possibly find a job in another state, but there is still no guarantee of better conditions anywhere else.

The welfare situation, which will be discussed more fully later, and the workmen's compensation laws do very little to relieve the problem. First of all, welfare money is limited and just barely provides a subsistence level type of existence. The compensations laws are set up proportionately to the individual's income, so, if a person had a very low income, his compensation benefits would be extremely low. Also, compensation laws do not provide for menial types of labor. What we have then, is those that are in the poorest of jobs and who need the money the most get the least (5, p., 39).

The small farmer who can no longer compete with the larger farms is forced to move into the cities. Of course, we hear a lot about the various types of parity, but they are for those farms which can produce a large market crop. The small farmer receives very little, if any, of those benefits. Again, we have the problem of those who need it the most get the least.

The elderly people who live in poverty may have been poor or they may have had a long illness which put them into the

culture of poverty. Many of the aged found in
poverty are women. They are widowed and left to live out
the remainder of their lives at barely a subsistence level.
It is no wonder these people contribute to the despondency
of the culture of poverty. These people get only a few dollars
a month, with no other income. Social Security is based upon
the individual's wages, and most of these people had low paying
jobs to begin with. Medical expenses take up what little of the money
that is not spent for food or housing. As society progresses there is
no hope for these people to progress. [Social Security has improved,
but is intended to be a portion of an individual's retirement. Medicare
is deducted from SS at $135 per month per person. A supplement is also
required for another $50 per month plus co-pays for visits and
medications. This does not usually include dental or optometry.]

Others that are in the culture of poverty are the "disor-
ganized individuals." These are the ones we see most. They
are the alcoholics, bums, beatniks, and addicts. These people
are past the point of helping themselves struggle out of the gutter
(with the exception of the Beatniks.) They have
become slaves to alcohol and drugs, which now has all power
over them.

The people that live in this culture develop a personality
of poverty. They don't plan ahead, they are suspicious, they
tend to develop a fatalistic outlook on life, depression becomes a common state of mind, they begin to feel that it is
futile to try to get out of their conditions, and they develop extreme
pessimism. "…American culture, by assigning to each
individual responsibility for his own economic fate, encourages
feelings of guilt and self-blame among those who fail. These

feelings in turn serve an important social function since they focus criticism upon the individual Rather than upon those institutions and social organization which make success difficult for members of some groups to achieve." (8, p.,55).

Urban Renewal projects have attempted to deal with the housing situation of the slums. Housing is not getting at the real problem of slums but is actually making it tougher on a certain number of people in the poverty zone. One of the urban renewal projects that was set up, provided housing for 7 families. However, the buildings that were torn down displaced 10 families. The families which could not find housing in the new development were forced to move in with relatives or had to move into more crowded and worse conditions than had previously existed. [Currently called gentrification.]

The urban renewal projects are classic examples of how the culture of poverty operates. In these new projects there is still a high rate of personal crimes, such as, murder, theft, and rape. This housing project has only attacked one portion of the culture of poverty. Nothing has been done to relieve their meager incomes, or to better the educational system, and numerous other aspects of the culture of poverty have not been attacked. No one has attempted to change their outlook on life, or to give them some ambition for self-betterment. They just built new houses. As Harrington said in <u>The Other America</u>, "Perhaps the most important point to have emerged in this description of the Other America is the fact that poverty in America creates a culture, a way of life, and feelings, that it makes a whole society. It is crucial to generalize this idea for it profoundly affects how one moves to destroy poverty." (5, p.,156).

So, the urban programs have failed to attack the basic problem,
which is the culture that develops out of poverty. Thus,
we have merely moved poverty into better housing and expect
these people to start a whole new way of life.

We recognize the fact that these people are not
poor by their own choice, but they have no control over their
poverty. Poverty will not be abolished until there is a social
movement, which will affect the values and policies in other areas
of society that will allow poverty to become a thing of the past.

All too often we tend to think that those in the under-privileged
classes are taken care of by the welfare state.

Julius Horwitz points out several limitations of the typical
welfare agency caseworker and the facilities he is given to
work with. Not only are welfare people inadequately providing
for the poor, but the poor are being exploited by those around them.

On the national level the poor are the last to be provided
for. They have no political voice which is willing to speak on their
behalf. They constitute no threat to the strong political parties. They are not educated and are not organized
enough to speak for themselves. An example of this is the fact
that a bill proposed during the first part of the Kennedy
administration would have provided adequately for the small
farmer I mentioned. There were also clauses concerning
minimum wage laws that would have benefited the urban worker.
However, the strong Farm Bureau opposed the bill and so did other
conservative forces. The result was the passing of a substitute

bill that provided for only 50,000 people, when the problem
concerned millions (5, p., 60).

At the municipal level there is a more direct type of
exploitation of the poor. The housing which these people are
forced to live in is terrible. In the larger urban areas
there may be several people living on one floor of an apartment
building. They must share one or two bathrooms between several
of them, and the same type of an arrangement is made for the
kitchen. The landlords, in some cases, have made one fairly
good-sized room into small rooms by partitioning it into two
sections. Yet, they will charge the same rent for each small room
that they charged for the fairly large room. The houses
are on the border line of being condemned, but yet, such buildings are
allowed to exist despite building codes. The inspectors may demand that
the landlord make repairs, but the landlord just fulfills
the barest necessities to keep the building from being condemned.

Bribery and pay-offs to the police and the inspectors make it
even more difficult to get decent living conditions. We are quick to
criticize the police for such actions, but they are given the lowest of
pay and the toughest of circumstances, and we expect them to remain
infallible. [The problem still exists today! I underlined them because
of the current relevance.]

The men and women who are dedicated to the welfare agencies
are given a bare minimum to work with. They are underpaid, over-
worked, understaffed, and often they are untrained. A conversation
in The Inhabitants, demonstrates these facts.
A case worker who was concerned for his own family as well as

those in his casebook. He had this to say about his income:

> "This book is the papa for 35,000 people right here
> in New York City getting assistance. And I'll bet my pay that There
> are tens of thousands of people right here in New York who don't
> even live up to the minimum standards that we lay down, but who
> would rather eat old newspapers than apply for welfare…We're not
> giving what's necessary, we're just giving what's minimum…Do you
> know why I've been studying this manual, because my actual take
> home pay is below the minimum of what I could get if I went
> downstairs and signed an application." (6, p.,72). [Not a
> complaint, but I worked for the Easter Seal Society for 4 years and
> I was still eligible for Food Stamps. Social worker types do that.]

The caseworkers are given such caseloads that they cannot
hope to give anything, but the barest minimum of time to each
case. In places such as, New York they can only hope to see
their cases once every few months.

The caseworkers are not only required to work in the field, but they
have a considerable amount of paperwork which takes
a fair amount of their time. They must file forms on each
item they give to a case. They fill out extensive appli-
cations for the needs of their cases. Case records must be
kept on each individual, not to mention the numerous letters which must
be written to various agencies for further assistance or for housing,
employment, and other needs of their cases.

The caseworker must deal with his own responses to his
cases. He faces many frustrations and few triumphs, in most cases. The
caseworker cannot hope to provide a great amount of goods for these
people, but the minimum is all that he can give. He is providing at a
minimum level so these people cannot be taken advantage of at the
national, municipal, and local levels. The caseworker is caught in the
middle. On top are those who exploit the poor and below are those living
in a culture that has no aspirations or ambitions and yet he is trying to
pull them out of the filth.

The slums are just one type of social problem. John Steinbeck, in his book, <u>The Winter of Our Discontent</u>, deals with those social problems that create the other America.

Steinbeck begins the book by the typical family observing the Easter season. These people exemplify the Christian ideals and ethics that the middle-class people proudly display on Sunday morning. Our social values make us regard these Christian ethics as important to our integrity and self-respect. The ideal of honesty, democracy, and fair play are also regarded as virtues of the American personality.

Ethan Hawley, the main character in the book, believed in these ideals, until he looked about himself and saw that the main motivating force in society was the monetary value. The banker was motivated purely for monetary reasons, as was the judge who had been fixing traffic tickets so long that he forgot it was dishonest. The Chief of Police knew very well of the corruption, but he could do nothing because he was part of it. There were just a few gray lines which made the difference between dishonest and just a little bit dishonest. It was an accepted value to be a little bit dishonest.

Ethan adopted these values as his own. He decided that the things that a few little dishonesties could bring would be worth it. After all, he would become honest again after he just did it once. These little shady deals were not crimes against anyone, they were crimes against money. The men who governed the town politically, morally, and economically had been so set in their ways for so long that they did not consider their activities illegal. They were normal men so how could a few slight deals make them immoral?

Marullo, the Italian immigrant, came to this country firmly believing in the Constitution; he'd memorized the Bill of Rights, and the Declaration of Independence and knew the words on the Statue of Liberty. He was chiseled out of all his money when he first came to this country. He learned from this, the true American values. He soon developed the philosophy of "Look out for number one." In his conversation with Ethan he revealed a true statement about the American people in general. "Everybody steals, some more, some less…" (12, p., 150). Marullo showed that the American ideals are not what they are publicized to be, they are monetary and looking out for number one.

Ethan's son exemplifies the attitude of our society. According to Chinoy, "To a large extent the individual can be considered a product of his society and culture," (3, p., 50).

After it was discovered that Allen had plagiarized his entry in the "I Love America Contest," Ethan confronted him with his conduct. Allen replied, "Who cares? Everybody does it. It's the way the cooky crumbles." "…Don't you read the papers? Everybody is in it right up to the top. You get to feeling holy, just read the papers" (12, p., 294).

Steinbeck was trying to point out that Allen is the product of our society, he has learned the social values just as the child born into the culture of poverty accepts those values with which he is associated.

The real tragedy of the values and attitudes that Steinbeck points out is the fact that these values contribute to the poverty of the other America. Our monetary values have led to the exploitation of the poor. The most prominent men in the community pay such poverty-stricken people ridiculously low wages. We have seen how they have no political voice and are therefore not provided by legislation to any great extent. The attitude that we have to look out for number one leaves no one to look out for those who can't help themselves. Juvenile delinquency is the harassment of mother's clubs everywhere. The mothers of the neighborhood are out scouting the newsstands and T.V. programs to make sure their children are not subjected to too much violence. They tend to feel the mass media is the "sure" cause for the rise of delinquency. Other favorite reasons for the cause of delinquency include:

> Too many mothers working
> Need more money for juvenile services
> There is no discipline in the home
> Need more psychiatric help
> Unsatisfactory schools
> Lack of religious training
> Poverty
> Broken homes
> Unemployment
> Need to get tough
> We should punish the parents for the child's crime
> We need to get the kids out of the city…

and the list goes on.

There is no agreement among the experts as to what the cause of delinquency is, but the most accepted theory is the multiple factor theory: That is, all of these causes are interdependent variables. Working at a society level, if one of the factors changes, then all the others must also change. There may be a specified single theory, but it must take into consideration its relationship to the other factors.

There is not a 100% certainty of any theory that is proposed, but by using those factors and common sense, the prediction of the cause is little better than 60%.

To determine the actual number of delinquents there are in the U.S. is extremely difficult. There are only two agencies which report juvenile delinquent statistics, The Children's Bureau and the F.B.I. Also, another fact that makes the statistics inaccurate is the fact that in some states what might constitute delinquency, does not necessarily constitute delinquency in another state. So, when we try to analyze statistical relationships so as to determine the cause of delinquency there are more than just a few problems.

Tunley's theory of juvenile delinquency advocates that delinquency is the price we pay for progress. He contends that the change which goes along with progress causes anxiety in delinquents. Chinoy labels this "Unanticipated consequences of social action" (3, p., 46).

The correct remedy for delinquency is as evasive as the exact cause of delinquency.

The first method to remedy delinquency I shall deal with is The psychological approach. By this approach the child is Considered sick and is not responsible for his actions. "A wide-spread conception of youth is that they are neurotic, emotionally disturbed or in some way, maladjusted" (13, p.,125-126). The psychological method does have its advantages in some cases. Tunley mentioned that such an approach is only good in 10% of the delinquent cases. Therefore, this is not one of the main remedies.

The sociological approach seems to be the popular approach to remedying delinquency. There are cries for slum clearance, adequate housing, numerous playgrounds, equal opportunities for jobs and etc., which are supposed to solve the problem. I previously pointed out that the crime rate was just as high in the new housing developments and said that it had little effect upon delinquency. The housing developments put all of the failures, welfare cases and the uninspired together in a community with seemingly no future. The few talented who do emerge with an adequate income must move out of the development because of the income ceiling, which says anyone over a certain income level must move out. The leadership of the community is drained off. The children do not develop respect for anyone in the community and in most cases they have no one to identify with.

The Negro population in the institutions is much higher than the ratios of the Negro population in the nation. The institution population is 33 to 67, while the

national ratio is only 11 to 89. Those social values which are
causing poverty, the Negro problem, are probably resp- onsible
for the high ratio of Negro crime.

Our educational system is making somewhat the same mistakes the
housing projects made. We are forcing kids with below average
I. Q.'s to remain in school until they are sixteen.
our educators feel they are helping to solve the delinquency
problem, by keeping the kids off the streets. However, in many
cases the child will fail to gain anything from this type of
education beyond the age of thirteen, but he is required by law
to remain in school until he is sixteen. We have developed the
attitude that unless we have a middle-class education it is un-
American. The child becomes frustrated that he cannot do the
average work. He sits for three, or so, years biding his time
until he can finally get out. During this waiting period,
frustrations develop and the child will become a disciplinary
problem. Truancy will increase and the afternoons after school
will be spent doing something more exciting. Most of these
delinquents have trouble reading. Since schoolwork depends heavily
upon reading skills, this is the main area of frustration at
school.

This summer, while working at the Luther Burbank School for
Boys, I became familiar with this problem of the school vs. the
delinquent. The boys are required to attend school while they
are at the institution. Most of the boys have difficulty with
school subjects and would rather do anything than go to school.

The one subject that all the boys liked was the shop class. On the days that the boys went to shop class there was actually a change in their behavior for the rest of the day. Some of the boys, even though they may function at the 13-year-old level when they are 15, are very creative in building projects. Maintain- ance work was much preferred to school subjects, and the problem of frustrations does not exist in such activities.

As Tunley cited, 27.5% of the children who attend our schools are handicapped mentally so they will never reach the average development level of their age. I agree with Tunley when he states that we should allow these children to leave school younger, or offer educational alternatives, such as vocational training, at an earlier age. However, this would mean we would have to change our social values of education and get rid of such thinking that vocational training for children is un-American. There could then be a practice of policy which would help remedy the delinquent problem.

Tunley criticized our institutional system for delinquents as being too large and too impersonal. I agree with him 100%. A child is taken from his environment and is put in an institution which is to provide a better environment. As it turns out, the child is put in an environment where he must be tough to survive. Kids from every walk of life and every type of prob- lem are thrown into this large storehouse for delinquents. However, there are token attempts made to rehabilitate these children.

The thing that amazed me the most was the fact that they would put
a child in an institution who had been committing delinquent acts for
six or seven years, and then they expect to rehabilitate him in less than
a year. The recidivism rate at Burbank, I was told, was quite low.
However, there were very few boys in the cottage that I worked in who
had not been in at least two other types of institutions. I drew my own
conclusion that the recidivism at Burbank was well above the 60% level.
The institutions abroad are based on the foundation that work is the
best therapy for delinquent children (13, p., 220). In my experience
there were very few boys who were not eager to help with work, especially
if they saw some future in it. Adolescents are at a strange age, where
they are trying hard to be an adult. The boys I worked with did not know
how to go about becoming an adult. Working became their link to responsibility, which was their pathway to becoming an adult. In our
institutions this desire is not given a chance to grow, unlike
institutions abroad, where work programs develop into apprenticeships for
the children, so they have some future when they
get out.

Another helpful program which our institutional organization is just now beginning to practice, is the use of the
half-way-home. A half-way-home is a small living group which
is structured after a regular family. The boy lives in this
environment for a certain amount of time before he is returned
to society. The home, as stated, is a regular home type of

situation. A couple act as the father and mother to a small group
of boys. The boys go to work or to school and then return to
the home in the evening where they have a home cooked meal and
are provided with the warmth of a real family. Without the
half-way-home there is nothing to keep the child from returning
to a life of crime once he leaves the institution. He is
usually placed in the same environment which contains those
factors which caused his delinquency in the first place.
The half-way-home provides a transition from the institution to
society. The home will give him a good start in helping him
overcome his problems. In some of the homes the recidivism
rate has been as low as 4% or 5%, while on the over-all average,
the rate is extremely lower for those who have attended the
homes, than for those who have not had this advantage (13, p.,243-245).

Several remedies are suggested by Tunley, but he asks,
"Are we willing to pay the price?" Are we willing to pay for
work programs, to change our values of education, will we
raise the salaries of those working with delinquents?
These are just a few prices we must pay if we are to remedy the
problem of delinquency.

From my own point of view, I found that Merullo's
philosophy, of looking out for number one, increased the
problems of the delinquents. No one was looking after them, so
they did whatever it took to please number one. In the institution the majority of the staff are looking out for themselves,
from the supervisor down to the painter. (I would like to do a

paper someday, on the subject of personalities of the
penal institution staff.) The kids seemed to be secondary to
many of the staff members, who gained ego fulfillment by the
domination of the kids.

By the end of the summer I found that the best way to get
a positive reaction from the kids was to show them that somebody did
give a damn about them. In the movie, "Manhattan Battleground,"
the social worker genuinely expresses his concern for the people
and kids in the neighborhood, and he greatly affected the
lives of many of them. It is this type of attitude it takes to
get through to delinquents. The results are not immediate, and
it may take a long time to get to even one boy, but the results
are far greater, in my opinion, than anything else that could
be done for them. This is a simple form of remedy which, if
practiced by all of those associated with delinquents, could
help reduce the rate of recidivism. Since any drastic change
in the institutional format will be a long time in coming, I
would like to propose this simple remedy of genuine concern, which could
be put into effect immediately, if we so desired.

On May 2nd 1960, Caryl Chessman was executed. Before his
death he left a lasting impression on many Americans for some
time to come. His book, _Cell 2455 Death Row_, caused a controversy
that was heard around the world. That controversy was about
"capital punishment."

Chessman, in his book, created an image of a boy who seemed
to be a victim of circumstances. The boy was racked with illness
which left him with the loss of a musical genius he once had.

Then tragedy struck his family, and he began stealing food to help with the family income. Society was cruel and there was no attempt to understand his motives, but he was declared wrong by society, and therefore, he must be punished. In his revolt against society he led a life of crime, which put him in one institution after another. Chessman pointed out the faults of the institutions and noted how they did not rehabilitate, but merely were places to stay until he could get back on the streets. Eventually, his life of crime led him to the gas chamber for the kidnapping and molesting of two women. [He Denied the charges]

Through the long legal process that determined that he was to die, the notes of the original trial became confused as a result of the death of the court stenographer. He was how-ever, condemned to die. Thus, the debate on capital punishment began. Did society have the right to condemn a man to die when there may possibly have been a mistake in the court proceedings? And doesn't society have the responsibility to rehabilitate those individuals who are victims of circumstances? Since society was partly at fault should he die?

Some of the arguments for capital punishment include:

1. Capital punishment provides a deterrent for crime.
2. The threat of capital punishment gives police protection.
3. Society is protected from the violent people
4. The reformation of the convicts is unlikely.
5. Retribution must be made for crimes committed.
6. Capital punishment is church sanctioned.

Arguments against:

1. Statics show that capital punishment is not a deterrent.
2. Racial, economic, and sex factors may be the cause of bias in the selection for capital punishment
3. There is a possibility of jury fallibility.

4. There is no way to revoke the sentence of the
   innocent once the person has been executed.
5. Reformation of the prisoner is possible and more
   desirable.
6. There is a shared guilt by all the members of society.
7. The idea of punishment is contrary to the penological
   theory of rehabilitation.

In the last election, Oregon witnessed a change in policy, due to the change in social values regarding capital punishment. The Oregon voters, in the last election, were given the opportunity to vote on a referendum which would abolish capital punishment in Oregon and it passed. If we review the history of capital punishment we can see how the social attitudes have changed in Oregon.

1903—Changed from county to state executions
1912—4 were hanged at once
1914—Capital punishment was abolished by 157 votes
1920—Capital punishment was reinstated by 17,000 votes
    (This was due to the public opinion that was aroused
     by the brutal slaying of two prominent Oregon
     citizens in 1920.)
1937—Gas chamber replaced hanging
1955—Law passed which provides for an automatic appeal
    of the death sentence to the Oregon Supreme Court.
1958—Voted against abolishing capital punishment by
    12,000 votes, or 2% of the total vote
1962—58th person executed since 1903
1963—Four were condemned to die, Herbert Mitchell 41,
    Richard Schwensen 29, Larry Shipley 22, and
    Jeannace Freeman 21.
1964—Nov. 4th the referendum was passed which abolished
    capital punishment, by a vote of 439,495 to 291,137.

The passing of the referendum expressed the attitude of the Oregon voters. They apparently felt that the arguments against capital punishment outweighed those for it. Chessman believed that his life would not be taken in vain, because the controversy he caused would force a conscious decision concerning capital punishment upon the people. He felt that the history of his case would have a bearing upon the cases of those who would come after him (4, p., 671). This apparently held true for the Oregon voters. I feel that the controversy his case caused did influence the Oregon voting.

The Negro problem in this country stems from the importation of slaves during the early years of the country. The Negro was thought to be the handy man and nothing more. The Negroes were expected to live separately, but not equally. When the Negro realized that he was not living equally to the white man he could do nothing about it. He was afraid of the white man. The entire legal structure was against the Negro, and he had no way to better his lot. The Negro found himself being exploited by the white man. They are forced to pay high rent, the teachers are forced to teach in inferior educational systems, they had to endure cruel police brutality and due to discrimination they are forced to live in filth and disease.

The Negroes, when they first came, were squeezed together into ghettos where they were taught the white man's education. They had no texts dealing with their culture, so they passed on their culture to their generations. They developed their own religion, they had their own language and jargon and in short, they were a cultural group. However, they were forced together by negative forces, and there forged their culture together as the result of the white man's discrimination (7, p., 63-64). Discrimination is the acting out of prejudice. Prejudice develops from basically three different, but related sources. The First source is cultural or learned. Discrimination is practiced in the community by the "white only" signs. People assume that

if there are no Negroes in town then it follows logically
that they shouldn't be there. People see the Negroes in
menial jobs only, they see them in the slum areas, and these are the
only contact people have with the Negroes and this contributes
to the establishing of prejudices.

Prejudice then develops into an ideology of racism. Racism
was developed in the 19th century to keep the Negroes in
slavery, which was necessary to the economy at that time.
To rationalize the democratic ideal, the idea developed that
the Negroes were an inferior race and couldn't engage in full
citizenship. This ideology has been passed on from generation
to generation and is present today.

The second theory of prejudice advocates that it develops
at the social, or group, level. The competition for scarce values
promotes prejudice as does the competition for the three P's,
power, prestige, and possessions. If it is within the interest
of a group to promote prejudice instead of letting the Negroes
compete for these same values, then, discrimination follows.
Racism developed in the U.S. out of the possessions struggle and
economic reasons. In Germany racism was promoted for political
power.

The third theory of prejudice is the psychological approach.
Frustration and aggression develop and these form a need of
release from the individual, which leads to a "scapegoat."
Aggression and frustration cannot be taken out on a source such as
authority, or stronger elements in society, so we look
for a weaker element in society for a scapegoat. The Scapegoat

must be weaker, identifiable, and visible. Therefore, minority racial groups provide a perfect scapegoat.

There is a symbolic element attached to the selection of a scapegoat. If it is economic frustration the individual is experiencing, then the Jew will be selected because they are the prominent businessmen. If the frustration is sexual, then the Negro will be selected, because of the folklore about the sex potency of the Negro.

Our defense mechanisms cause further prejudice. Projection is a form of repression, whereby, we project our own desires and activities onto another group. If an explanation of a con-fusing situation is needed we develop the single factor theory, because it is easy to pick out one single group. Furthering prejudices is the need for self-esteem. No matter how low our image may be of ourselves, we must have someone that is still lower to have any self-esteem at all. The authoritarian personality adds to this by the need to dominate and rule over others. And finally, at the psychological level, there is the individual who has an actual neurosis and feels he has to react to a certain group in a specific way.

In the <u>Negro Revolt</u>, it was brought out that the discri-miation in housing and employment were the most important areas of discrimination caused, once again, by prejudice.

At the housing level the Negroes are charged higher prices than the whites, but they are given poorer housing. They are forced to congregate in a ghetto and often the rent is so high that families must double up in the same apartment.

The children are forced to go to a school which is inferior
in educational equipment. Even if the school is technically
integrated, the school boundaries almost invariably make it
an entire Negro school, which still gets the poorest of facilities. The ghetto becomes a health hazard; there is a direct
correlation between this type of crowded housing and poor
health. These neighborhoods increase welfare costs for the
entire community, because they cannot get jobs and since the
rent for Negroes is higher, and the welfare agency must
provide the money. If the Negroes attempt to move out of the
ghetto and into a white neighborhood, that neighborhood will
turn into a ghetto because the white population will leave if
the Negroes become dominant (7, p., 68).

Job discrimination forces the Negro into poverty. He is
allowed to have only the menial jobs which have a low pay
scale. Society develops the prejudice that this is the only
job the Negro is suitable for, and so he is frozen into the
menial job role by the rest of society (11, p., 51).

The Negro cannot go into business because he has no capital,
in most cases, with which to invest. If a Negro is fortunate
enough to save enough money so that he may go into business he
must usually rent from the white man. There is usually a gentleman's
agreement between the shop owners as to the
amount of rent for Negroes.

Here again we see the values of the middle-class society pointed out
by Steinbeck. The amount of white collar crime

which was brought out in <u>Social Disorganization in America</u>,
displays the ethics of business; "…Businessmen customarily
feel and express contempt for law, and government. They
restrict and impede the businessman's behavior" (8, p., 163).

Our society today has created prejudice and discrimination
from our social values of possessions. We are willing to pay
the price for possessions which is, the Negro problem.

The Negroes are discriminated against at every level of
society. This economic straight-jacket breaks down the
family and promotes the general lowering of morality. This
break down is the fundamental cause of Negro crime. The
Negroes turn to crime to gain those material possessions which
they cannot even work for. Dope addiction becomes an escape from the
ghetto. Prostitution becomes a way of life, and the
social values of immorality and degradation become the
accepted standards for survival.

The organizations which have turned to legalism to help
fight the problem of racism have been greatly discouraged.
The Negroes had hoped to use legalism as a weapon to bring
about social change. The segregation laws for schools show
how slow legalism takes. Organizations such as NAACP, CORE,
SCLC and others were making progress, but they were too slow
for some Negroes.

The Student Non-Violent Coordinating Committee began the
sit-in demonstrations which developed a different type of
social movement to gain equality.

The Negroes who had at one time been afraid of the white
man were now demonstrating with alarming boldness.

The movement of the SNICK group has been accepted as a new religion forged out of 300 years of human suffering. The theology of the religion is desegregation. When the Freedom Singers visited our campus I couldn't help but feel that these people had been oppressed so long that they were going to spread their gospel, and once the movement began there was no turning back, whatever the cost. Maybe a bit of a dramatic parallel, but I could not help but think of the Christian movement and the Jewish exodus. Has the time come for the Negro?

At any rate, the most important element in giving the Negroes equal opportunities is to make them into responsible citizens. "Three hundred years of slavery and discrimination have destroyed the inner fiber of the American Negro" (7, p., 25). The Negro may be spiritually incapable of becoming first class citizens right now; so they must learn to be responsible with the rights they have been given. The Urban League is devoted to making Negroes into good citizens. They attempt to attack the crime rate, the inability to get jobs and they also attack those crimes which are caused out of frustrations such as dope and prostitution. The Negro must develop the responsibility of making proper use of political and economic forces to further his movement to end racism.

The Family is the basic institution of every society. In this paper we have been talking a lot about the effects of progress. Progress has also had its effect upon the family. Progress presents a rapid change of situations without giving anyone a chance to adjust including the family.

The family has become the last stronghold for intimacy.
Even within the family there is love and conflict at the
same time. If the family is to survive this conflict of
problems, they must be solved within the general attitude of
love. There must be an acceptance and complete forgiveness
without retribution.

Our society effects this family which is trying hard to
remain intimate, despite the elements of conflict. The authority within the family is broken down. The father is at work
all day and the mother is home most of the time, so there
is a cold war between the mother and father for authority in
the family. The mother becomes the central figure in the
family because she is always in the home, while father is
just the person who brings home the check.

The father must be returned to the head of the family.
He must take part in the child's discipline from the start,
and the simple act of letting the father distribute the allow-
ance will give the father a certain amount of respect in the
eyes of the child. The father then becomes the child's link
with the outside world. The child thus determines that the
father is the provider, and not the mother. The mother should
add to the stability of the family by becoming the organizer of
leisure time activities. She must also develop roots
within the neighborhood and community to round out the family.

The generational relations today are more strained than
ever. The revolt of the adolescent in today's family can cause

a split in the family relations. The aged are also a problem. They often have to live with the young couple, or receive some support from the couple which might limit their own finances. The aged no longer are respected for the virtues of their age, as they are in other societies.

To curtail the rebellion of the young, there should be a proper balance of authority within the family. The father and mother should both set definite limitations for the child. The parents must ease the child's transition from the protective family to the outside world. To reduce anxiety that is built up in the child, the family should establish cooperative relationships with the school, church and the neighbors.

The aged should not become isolated from the nucleus of the family, but should strengthen intimacy and family ties. We should cultivate a respect for the aged within our children. There should be social legislation which would allow the aged to have financial independence as this would greatly ease family strains.

The family must seek to establish personal integrity and responsibility within the young. The schools, churches, or neighborhood are unable to do this alone. The family should cultivate these human values at an early age, through family contacts and community contacts.

Ethan Hawley, in Steinbeck's book, failed to do this with his son. He hoped to return to his family and wanted to develop these human values in his daughter.

Several of the problems that our complex society creates are known as forms of withdrawal or escapes from the pressures of living.

The forms of withdrawals at the social perspective level in order of seriousness are:

    Compulsive smoking
    Compulsive gambling
    Compulsive drinking
    Drug addiction
    Mental illness
    Suicide

The problem of addiction, like the other forms of withdrawals, is of a social nature. The reason people become addicts cannot be generalized, except that it is usually due to some personal problem from which the individual seeks to withdraw by the use of drugs.

Once the addict becomes addicted, the withdrawal symptoms from the drug are so severe that the addict will do anything to avoid these symptoms. Once the habit takes a strong hold on the addict, he becomes a slave to the drug. To support the habit, the addict is quite often forced to a life of crime to meet the price of the drug that he must have.

Our narcotic laws have made it exceedingly hard to deal with the problem. The narcotics racket is forced into the underground, and all those who cannot support their habits through legal sources, such as doctors, must become, by definition, an enemy of society.

Addiction is a disease. When the body builds up a tolerance to the drug, the body cannot function properly without

the drug in the system. This may be defined as a disease.
However, the important disease in addiction is the problem
which causes the addict to seek withdrawal by the use of the
drug.

When an addict is forced to take a cure for addiction he is sent to
Lexington where there is a hospital for addicts. The addict may kick the
habit, but when he goes back to the same environment that he came from he
usually resorts to the use of the drug again. Thus, having once kicked the
habit and the body is adjusted to living without it, the addict may still
rely upon the drug. This leads us to believe that addiction is also a
disease of the mind.

The other forms of withdrawal that were listed have
therapeutic organizations that help the individual, such as
Alcoholics Anonymous, Gamblers Anonymous, and etc. These groups
consist of patients who gather to help cure themselves. Since
the Alcoholics Anonymous group is probably the best organized, by seeing
their program we can understand how they help the individual and how
similar organizations operate.

1.   The person is re-socialized, because alcoholism
      isolates the individual.
2.   The problem is defined as an illness rather than the
      lack of will power.
3.   This type of therapy is more likely to help the
      social-going type of personality who can accept the
      treatment on a give-and-take emotional basis.
4.   There are twelve steps which the alcoholic believes
      in. These steps create psychological attitudes which
      are therapeutic.

In our Social Psychology class last Fall semester, we learned that
the alcoholic had certain psychological components.

These components of the alcoholic are:
1. High anxiety of personal relationships
2. Emotional immaturity
3. Ambivalence toward authority
4. Grandiose feelings (thinks he's a big shot)
5. Has a low self-esteem at the same time
6. Has feelings of isolation
7. Perfectionists, but can't meet their own perfectionism
8. Guilt feelings
9. Compulsiveness

The personality of an addict is probably similar to these components. The difference is that the addict chooses drugs, instead of alcohol, to withdraw from his problem. The laws we have passed to stop the traffic of narcotics, in hopes of stopping addiction, are just attacking the symptoms of the problem. The real problem is not addiction. An example: The narcotic racket flourishes in Harlem. The Negroes rely upon drugs to take them momentarily away from the ugliness of the ghetto. Yet, the laws are aimed at stopping the individual from taking the drugs, instead of passing laws which would forbid such filthy conditions to exist, which are the actual cause of the drug problem.

We can pass laws which would allow the addict to receive medical attention to kick the habit, but unless the underlying cause is solved, the addict would find another form of withdrawal which might be worse than addiction. I would disagree with Wakefield, in The Addict, that the best thing to do for the addicts is to provide increased medical care and legislation.

I think the addicts need psychological and sociological help more than anything else. We must start treating the cause rather than the symptoms.

Harrison Brown's book, <u>The Challenge of Man's Future</u>, deals with another type of problem. He deals with the physical environment problems, rather than social problems, but the social problems are greatly affected.

The price of progress is once again giving man a good deal to be concerned about. Our tremendous industrial growth is using up all of the natural resources at a rapid rate which man will suffer for in the future.

Those resources which were once on the surface of the earth are now found deep inside the earth [Fracking?] because all of the non-renewable natural resources have disappeared with advancement. In the future man will have to use different types of energy, such as, atomic, solar and others that science can develop.

Population demands are forcing the rapid use of the natural resources. More people mean that we need more progress [development]to provide for them. If we do not solve the problem of population we will not have to worry about any of those problems already mentioned in this paper. Even in the face of world over-population there are many obstacles in overcoming a widespread birth control program, say on an international level.

1. Religious opposition, belief that it is unethical
   to practice birth control. [I was not referring to abortion.]
2. The problem of literacy and general educational level
   of some countries would hamper such a program.
3. Fear and superstitions develop in connection with
   birth control.
4. Economic reasons, such as the cost of contraceptives,
   make it difficult for many countries to promote such
   a program.

5.   There may be no motivation to control the size of the
     family. In some cultures, it is a sign of virility to
     have many children.

Man is not looking into the future to see what problems over-population is really going to cause. Our resources are now being wasted with no foresight to conserve them. We will have to resort to atomic energy, solar energy and to those resources we can obtain by processing ordinary rocks.

If these problems are not solved, Brown says there will be three alternative results. The most likely is that we will revert back to an agrarian society as a result of war. There will be no technological advancement of machines, because the machinery will be destroyed by the war and there will be no more natural resources to support a great technological advancement. The second result may be a controlled, collectivized industrial society where the conduct of men, as well as the natural resources will be carefully guarded. The third, and most improbable result might be a free world-wide industrealized society where men live together in harmony, if we solve all the problems of population, war, and etc. Brown admits that this type of society could probably not exist for any great length of time (1, p., 264).

In conclusion to the social problems, I would like to say that the middle-class values, and ideals which are accepted as a way of life in the middle-class are expressed by Steinbeck quite accurately. It is these values that are contributing to all the other social problems. Those in the culture of poverty are exploited by the middle-class people. The middle-class attitudes towards education, institutions, and the causes of

juvenile delinquency are actually contributing to the problem.
The Negroes are discriminated against, but this has almost
become an institution in our society. In our passing of
narcotic laws we are actually persecuting the addicts for something they have no control over. We are attacking the symptoms
of the problem. It is the social values and attitudes of the
middle-class which are causing most of these problems. Are
we willing to pay the price of these problems for a few self-
centered values? I think not. There is an increasing awareness
on the part of the people to do something about these problems,
and I can't help but have an optimistic outlook for man's future.

As for an evaluation of the course, the course presented
in this manner gave a better understanding of the problems.
There was more work in this type of a course, as compared to
a textbook course, but it was most stimulating and eye opening.
The books were excellent, except for, <u>Love and Conflict</u>,
which I didn't enjoy as much as the others because of the Biblical
interpretations the author gave to everything.

One of the drawbacks of the course, I felt, was that a
discussion leader should have been chosen for each book before
we came to class, so we could have had better organized dis-
cussions.

Another drawback was the fact that we are graded only on one
paper. I wouldn't mind being graded on one paper if we
were given either a passing or failing grade. It's the distributing of the
grades A,B,C, and so on that I object to.

This is one course I felt as though I really benefitted and
learned a lot from, but yet my grade is determined by how I express what I
have learned in one paper. Then it is up to
the professor to read all of the papers and decide which one
of the fine lined categories I belong in, A,B,C,D, or F.
My style of writing, use of grammar and several other factors that go into
the grading of this paper are not indicative of
what I have actually learned in the course. As I said before,
I wouldn't mind this method if we were just given passing
and failing grades, but our educational system is built
around grades.

<u>Bibliography</u>

1. Brown, Harrison, <u>The Challenge of Man's Future</u>,The
        Viking Press, New York, c. 1954.

2. Chessman, Caryl, <u>Cell 2455 Death Row</u>, Pocket Books
        Inc. U.S., 1956.

3. Chinoy, Ely, <u>Sociological Perspective</u>, Random House,
        New York, c. 1954, 12th printing June 1963.

4. Cogley, John, "Capital Punishment," <u>Commonweal</u>,
        March 18, 1960.

5. Harrington, Michael, <u>The Other America</u>, Penguin
        Books Inc., Maryland, c. 1962.

6. Horwitz, Julius, <u>The Inhabitants</u>, The New American
        Library, New York, c. 1960.

7. Lomax, Louis, <u>The Negro Revolt</u>, The New American
        Library, New York, c. 1962.

8. McGee, Reece, <u>Social Disorganization in America</u>,
        Chandler Publishing Co., San Francisco, c. 1962.

9. <u>Oregonian</u>, Oregonian publishing, Wed. Nov. 4, 1964.

10. <u>Oregonian</u>, Orgonian publishing, Thurs. Nov. 5, 1964

11. Raab, Earl, editor, <u>American Race Relations Today</u>,
        Doubleday and Company Inc. New York, c. 1962.

12. Steinbeck, John, <u>The Winter of Our Discontent</u>,
        Bantam Books, New York, c. 1961.

13. Tunley, Roul, <u>Kids, Crime and Chaos</u>, Dell Publishing
        Co., Inc., New York, c. 1962.

14. Wakefield, Dan, <u>The Addict</u>, Gold Medal Books, Fawcett
        Publications, Inc. Conn. c.1963.

15. Winter, Gibson, <u>Love and Conflict</u>, Doubleday and
        Company Inc., New York, c.1958.

Epilogue

The problems of the '60's have followed us into 2020 with no amicable end in sight. The four months of protests in Portland and Seattle devolved early on into nightly riots with arson, looting, and even a few murders. The police are standing by. The only effective police presence came about as the result of the Proud Boys announcing that they would, more or less, stop the violence. The police showed up to protect the rioters from the "vigilantes." This was the most peaceful night so far. While decried as a white supremacy movement they are composed of all ethnic backgrounds.

In the meantime, I've posted a few, not too many, views on FB. I've learned this. Even a few people you count as friends can become acerbic, acquaintances get hostile, and friends of friends feel down-right entitled to call me a racist, hater, and the most benign label of all, "Old, Privileged, White, Guy." (If they really cared about me, they would mention that I am also Fat.)

On the final page of this tome I have printed for the reader, an old-fashioned Permission Slip to reverently refer to me as an Old Privileged, White [Fat] Guy. It does have some provisions. I plan to keep a few copies handy so when people think they are denigrating me with the OPWG moniker I will send/text or beat them about the head and shoulders with a rolled-up copy. Here Endeth my Rant, which is my new literary genre to, well…Rant. How else can I politely respond to impolite Ranters?

Intentionally Left Blank for your own notes

The Oregonian, Sunday June 7, 2020 **C5**

Coach Durham's 1965 team stood together against racism

Leroy Fails (20) and his Linfield teammates celebrate a victory in the 1965 NAIA semifinals. *Courtesy of Linfield College*

Ken Goe *The Oregonian/OregonLive*

Odis Avritt had concerns, which is why he went to Linfield College football coach Paul Durham's office late in the fall of 1965.

Linfield had rallied to beat Sul Ross State and advance to the NAIA championship game against St. John's of Minnesota. Avritt was a Linfield running back.

The title game was in Augusta, Georgia, home of the famed Augusta National Golf Club and the Masters Tournament. It was deep in what then was the segregated South. Avritt is black.

"I never had been that far south in my life," Avritt says. "I'd read and heard about teams going down there, and teammates being split up. I wanted to know what was going to happen."

Durham heard him out before answering.

"Coach Durham said we're going there as a team and we will be staying together," Avritt remembers. "That was the end of it."

The Wildcats went to Augusta and all stayed in a hotel hosting the teams and NAIA officials. They lost the game and went back to get ready for an NAIA banquet and hall of fame induction ceremony in the hotel that night.

After Linfield's traveling party filed into the banquet room, some players noticed Durham talking to a hotel official and then making several trips into the kitchen.

"I wondered what in the world he was doing?" defensive lineman Bob Ferguson says. "What's Coach doing in the kitchen?"

When the food came out, it was served to everyone but the Linfield players, coaches and boosters.

Linfield had a 33-player traveling squad that included several black and Hawaiian players. Everybody was hungry, and a little taken aback.

Ferguson, Avritt and other Linfield players pieced it together later from those who overheard some uncomfortable conversations between Durham and the hotel staff.

"As Coach Durham was escorting our team into the banquet hotel, he was approached by the manager of the banquet area," Avritt says. "He said, 'Your black and brown players will have to eat in the kitchen.'

"I can't really say how that conversation transpired, other than Coach Durham's response was: 'Well, if those players have to eat in the kitchen, our whole team will eat in the kitchen.' Coach was informed: No, they couldn't serve the whole team in the kitchen. So, Coach Durham said, 'Well,

if you're not going to serve our whole team in the banquet area, then don't serve us.'"

The hungry players didn't hear it from Durham. He simply gathered them together after the banquet, pulled out his wallet, handed each one $5 and told them to find something to eat. People on the hotel staff told Linfield's black and Hawaiian players of a restaurant that would allow them inside. Avritt went with mixed feelings.

"I felt bad," says Avritt, who is retired and lives in Portland. "I guess I knew somewhere along the line something wasn't going to work out. I had that feeling.

"But I think Coach Durham lived up to his word to me. We were there as a team. That was reflected in his actions."

Ferguson, who is white, concedes he didn't think much about it at the time. In his mind, that was the South. That was how things were there then.

Over time, he says he has come to a greater understanding about how dehumanizing the experience had been for some of his teammates. He has come to believe Durham not only was backing his non-white players, he was teaching something to the entire team by standing on principle and living up to his word.

"It was later in life, we realized how much guts that took for him to do something like that," Ferguson says. "But it was so in his character."

Durham coached football at Linfield from 1948 to 1967 and started a streak of consecutive winning seasons that now stands at 64 years. He left for the University of Hawaii to be athletic director. He died in 2007. As the years passed, a number of his players wanted to ensure he didn't fade into history. They organized and raised money to have a monument of Durham put up on the Linfield campus. Details of his 1965 stand against racism are inscribed on the monument.

"He was a great individual," Avritt says. "He was early on in the Northwest Conference in bringing people of color to play on his team. He was always very forthright. He was a Christian. He lived to his morals."

Avritt played for Linfield again in 1966 and remains an active supporter of the school and the athletic program.

"But I've never been back to Augusta," Avritt says. "And I'm a golfer."

kgoe@oregonian.com; @KenGoe

A handout from my run for state representative in the early 70's. I spent $2,000. My opponent spent $12,000, and he was endorsed by all the newspapers. I lost by 400 votes. An enlightening experience about the morality or lack thereof in politics.

Walkin' The Talk

A few stories that need to be shared for my own self-aggrandizement. When I worked as a Group Life Supervisor at Luther Burbank School for Boys, I had a noteworthy experience that I have rarely shared. It's time.

Immanuel Forde was a ward of the state of Washington. His parents, relatives and even foster homes did not want him. He wasn't there for any crimes of violence like Garza, who had killed his parents, but for petty crimes and major incorrigibleness. I liked him. He was tall and gangly for 13 years of age. His skin was more brown than black, big feet, and long, lanky arms. I liked him. Despite his rudeness to other staff and kids, we got along. I think it was playing catch with the football and shooting a few hoops with him. There was no sass, but there were big toothy grins, and he liked to hear me tell about college football. I mentioned his skills might take him to college. When nobody else was around we had some talks about his abilities to succeed.

The summer of '64 passed quickly. My time at the school is chronicled in the Chicken Book, but the day I left the school is omitted, for whatever reason. As I headed out to my pickle green, '52 Chevy that I bought after I wrecked my DKW motorcycle, Immanuel came running out of the cottage door. Mr. Ferguson! Mr. Ferguson! I could hear the staff in the cottage yelling at him to get back to the dinner table. He was incorrigible. I liked him.

The kids could NEVER say anything nice to a staff member. It would be against all the rules of "Cool." He shocked me. He ran up and put his gangly arms around my waist in a hug. He blurted, "Mr. Ferguson, I sure do Hate you." The kids were incapable of expressing affection. What could I say? "Immanuel, I sure do Hate you too, but I'm going to miss you." "I couldn't let you go without telling you how much I Hate you," he said. I squeezed him harder. It was awkward, but in that moment the thought ran through me that if I were in a different circumstance, I might adopt him.

A staff member broke up our goodbyes by shouting "Get back in here Immanuel or I'll have to put you on report." We waved and it ended with me yelling. "I hope to see you when you get out of here." The staff member gave me a look that was either a glare or complete amazement like I had lost my mind, and for a few moments…I had.

Wardell and Bobby

Back in the 80's it was the norm for Manufactures Representatives to cover the 11 Western states. Most were one-man businesses. I covered only OR, WA, ID, MT, and AK. I wanted to expand, but wanted to do the job right. When I took on the 11 states, I decided to hire reps in the Los Angeles area since California produced the most commissions of any state in the country. I called a few customers and they recommended Wardell and Bobby.

Wardell was the boss of a two-man shop and I knew we could recruit new lines to represent to make it a win-win business for all of us. I had morphed from representing athletic sporting goods companies (none you've ever heard of, they made gym shorts and uniforms,) to Advertising Specialty products (pens, pencils, and mugs with your name on them.) It worked like this; we would be assigned a territory; the 11 Northwestern states and we would receive a commission on any goods sold in the territory. The commissions were only 3% but with decent volume it made a great living. With more help, I felt we would attract more factories, called "lines" and make more money. It was our job to show the advertising goods to distributors. They were the businesses that eventually sold our products to the "end users" like Microsoft, Nordstrom's, and your local car dealers. It was low commissions, but high volume.

Wardell and I had several conversations and sealed the deal. He and his cohort, Bobby would get 80% of the commissions from California from all of our lines. It meant good money for them.

There was an annual Ad Specialty trade show in LA. It was gigantic and I would showcase Wardell and Bobby to my current lines at the morning sales meetings held at their booths. We would also interview together for new lines. I was thrilled.

Wardell picked me up at LAX . He told me what kind of car to look for and I told him what I was wearing. The suspect car stopped, the door opened, and I hopped in. We shook hands. He hadn't told me, but I suspected from his distinct elocution that he might be a person of color. We liked each other, but to end the awkwardness I said, "I don't know all the currently correct terms so how would you like me to refer to you as, a Negro, Black or African American?" His response was short and quick, with no trace of irritation, "How about Wardell." "That works for me!" That was the end of it.

Before the show opened, I planned to meet Wardell and Bobby at the booth of my best line. It was plastic coffee mugs and the like. They had just awarded me the CA territory based on my hiring two new people. I'm at the booth before anyone arrives. Wardell shows up. We chat while I pace back and forth waiting for Bobby. The sales manager for the manufacturer shows up. No Bobby. The show must go on, so we start the meeting. Bobby is 5 minutes late with a ton of excuses. He's well dressed and has a good gift of gab and convinces us all that his tardiness is justified. The rest of the day goes smoothly I've made a good decision.

We are interviewing for a major line the next morning. It would be a coup and a pot full of money to represent them. Bobby is late…but only 5 minutes. Again, plausible excuses. I am less than enthused. We wouldn't learn if we got the line until after the show. That night I buy their dinners. Bobby's on time.
I go on at great length the need to be on time, every time! The only thing we have to offer is better service.

Bobby is on time for the next meetings. I leave the show with high hopes. I give them a list of accounts to be contacted in the next few weeks. Wardell is diligent, Bobby is negligent. We did not get the big line I had hoped for. No problem. The first month I cut a check to their rep group. Wardell, being the leader of the two will have to pay according to his normal pattern. I get a call from Wardell and we discussed the Bobby situation. I did not want to put him on the spot to fire his partner and said I would do it if he wished. Wardell took it upon himself to let Bobby go. We worked together for a couple of years and then we split the sheets and I went back to repping in just OR, WA, ID, MT, and AK.

He was the first and only person of color that I ever saw in the Advertising Specialty business. We were not as successful financially as I would have hoped, but we became good friends. A few years after we split up, he called and asked me if I would represent him in the Sporting Goods business. I was flattered, but the Ad Specialty business was booming.

I am telling this story because I am not color blind, but I have demonstrated with my money, and more importantly, my business reputation that I "WALK the TALK!" Please think twice before you describe me with those misguided words, as a Privileged, Old, White Guy…and don't forget FAT!!

This homeless person just received a neck-scarf and a pair of socks handed out by a couple of us Pickleball players. The scarf was made by a gal and her grandkids. I've handed them out on the street in Portland and Vancouver. That's right, park the car, walk up to a person who looks a little down on their luck and ask them if they would like socks and a scarf. The response always reminds me of the adage "But for the Grace of God, There Go I." In 2019 we added socks we had contributed to the Portland Rescue Mission. We are not grandiose benefactors. We are the beneficiaries.

Good Cats

Close to ten years ago I got a call from an Ol' Linfield Wildcat. One of our Cats was in trouble, He, and his grandson for whom he was caring, were going to be evicted if he didn't have $1,800 by the next day.

I received the call at precisely 9:00 PM. We chatted about possibilities of how to raise the cash. We thought that 6 guys could pony up $300 each to resolve the crisis. I made a few calls. By 9:45 I had the money committed from a short list. We met the next day and the money was paid. Problem solved, (temporarily anyway.) The troubled Cat became more troubled. He left McMinnville and Linfield under duress. The money was not repaid as promised.

Now, some of the lenders were disgruntled that the money wasn't soon paid back. I've told them all these years, they may have lost $300 bucks, but we have a short list of guys we can call late at night to get bailed out. (I've since learned, by personal experience, that you can use a credit card for bail money, but that's another story.)

Nearly 10 years later, the friend who called me had received a check repaying the debt with interest. The episode was so ancient we couldn't quite remember who the Cat givers were. Our archaic brains pieced it together. The money was then given to Linfield naming the troubled Cat as the donor. As a result, the troubled Cat has been welcomed back to the school, is catching up with old Cats, and is back on social media. It took nearly a decade to come to fruition, but it is a story that warms the cockles of your heart…yes?

By now you are wondering why I am going on and on about a nice, but otherwise boring story. Because it's today's Headlines, but they are late!! There was NEVER a mention of the troubled Cat's race, but a bunch of Old Cats quietly proved a decade ago that Black Lives Matter. Call it, "Systemic Caring!" No accolades please, it's just who we are. Please don't call the press. They'd somehow make it all seem rather tawdry.

Should you feel entitled to describe me as a POWG also F, I will feel entitled to ask you this question, do you have a short list of friends who will bail you out despite your shortcomings? In fact, **I am asking** you that question right now. Take some time to take stock of your own circumstances.

PERMISSION SLIP

You are hereby given PERMISSION to call Bob Ferguson an Old Privileged, White Guy. If you wish to really be insulting, please include the obvious adjective, "Fat." Disclaimer, without stirring my ire, you need only include on your own resume ONE of the items listed from mine. They are:

1. Work for 4 years at a 501c3 of your choice at a wage that qualifies you for food stamps. My years as Director and fund-raiser for Camp Easter Seal, a camp for handicapped kids and adults was a Colossal experience. Hard work, meager earnings, but absolute Great Joy. Does Kaepernick qualify for meal assistance? You remember, the Nike darling who kneeled during the National Anthem and the media said, he "Sacrificed Everything," except for about $21 million? He is not allowed to call me an OPWG. I will accept pudgy

2. Promote, without fanfare, but at great personal expense in time and money, the building of a Monument to a great person who quietly lived his life in such a way that he could have written the sermons for MLK. I give you the Coach Paul Durham Plaza on the campus of Linfield University. His story is right where it deserves to be…etched in stone. It's worth the trip to McMinnville. The Oregonian recently printed the story of our '65 team due to its current relevancy.

3. Run for a public office or at least work on a political campaign. Everyone needs to know the debauchery that passes for "Just politics!" You will notice that I **NEVER** used the term "Fight" in my handout. In reality it's a mud-fight or worse.

4. Risk life and limb to serve your country and keep defenseless people from being slaughtered.

5. Hand out socks/scarves to the homeless on the street. Start with the ones in your drawer.

6. Have a story that demonstrates you have actually given a Dad-gum during your life.

7. Make your list of those who will bail you out. (Wives/husbands don't count.)

Per usual, I am open for a civil discussion and you may contact me at **robefergus@aol.com**.

The End

of Rudeness

Begins Here!

Addendum: No book is truly ever finished, and I found additional writings.

11/9/2020

Each Saturday, "The Columbian" newspaper publishes an editorial page with the title, **Cheers and Jeers.** They give **"Cheers"** to the stuff which, in their humble opinion, is good. They foist "Jeers" upon the bad actions of that week. The Equivalent in theater parlance, is a "rave" review or a "Pan," but with more maliciousness. They are entitled to such pronouncements because, well, after all…they are journalists reporting only the truth.

The Saturday page, while lengthy, is entertaining and usually spot-on. But in the article that I cited, they "missed the boat!!" I sent the following letter to the editor and in my own humble, but correct opinion, chastised them. In my memory, albeit not what it used to be, this is the only and there have been many, "Letter to The Editor" that I have ever written that has not been published. Shame on them!! I've even won an award which is very prestigious? (Some big **Cheers!** It has wormed its way into this second edition of "Social Problems.")

Jeers: In 1692 Salem had its **Witch Trials**, the **KKK** was founded in 1865, and 2020 has the Pandemic of **Covid 19** and a Pandemonium of "Social Problems!" They don't go away. They change players and morph into new forms.

Cheers: "We Shall Survive the Pandemic." (As I write this, 11/15/2020 a vaccine that is 90+ percent effective is being administered to those most in need.) The Current Chaos will abate, but never disappear.

Ba-Hum-Bug: As of 11/16/2020, The Columbian has not invited me, nor anyone else to gather "…under one tent…" to begin the conversation to remedy some of the social problems and "I ain't holding my breath," but maybe my term paper from 1965, "Social Problems" will get noticed?

Bob Ferguson

11/19/2019

To the Editor

Jeers: To the Columbian for missing an opportunity in your Cheers and Jeers section. Your article questions a legal/social system that gave a homeless man drug and mental health treatment instead of jail time after his 68th conviction. You squandered your chance to start a conversation for change, when you ended your opinion with "…69th chance seems a bit excessive."

I wrote a sociology paper 54 years ago at Linfield College. The nub of that tome was, "Why is there money for incarceration, but none for drug addiction or mental health care?" Decades later I now ponder a similar question, "Why wasn't there help for this person after his tenth conviction?" The man had been arrested 220 times and told "The Oregonian," "…he uses methamphetamines…it's easy to feel hopeless."

After the man's "Hopeless" statement, multiple arrests and 68 convictions prove that "Whatever we're doing Ain't working!" It's time for a deep shift in our legal/social system. The Columbian can rectify it own **Jeer.** You have the capacity to gather judges, politicians, and other influential citizens under one tent to begin the conversation for change. Please invite me.

3 Cheers: If you print my rant.

Bob Ferguson

Vancouver

A Dad-Gum shame this letter didn't make it into the paper. It is presented here as proof that I've been at this game for a while. To sum it all up I will leave you with this thought:

"When we drive people crazy, why are we surprised that they do crazy things?"

SUNDAY, JUNE 10, 2007

WINNING WORDSMITH

Each month we select a particularly good letter to the editor for special attention. The May winner is BOB FERGUSON, whose letter was first published on May 26. Ferguson is a K-8 substitute teacher with Evergreen Public Schools. His letter was selected because it offers an interesting and educational perspective on recidivism in the criminal justice system.

Let criminals reform

Forty-two years ago I was considering a profession as a counselor for juvenile delinquents. I wrote a senior thesis on the subject of recidivism. My conclusion was simple: Reduce the hopelessness of offenders and the speed of the revolving door will decrease. There are two barriers to a prisoner's success that can be removed right away that will have a substantial impact, and cost very little.

Bob Ferguson

The first is revising the draconian fine system. Fines are excessive and they compound at 12 percent per year, even when people are incarcerated with virtually no hope of payment. Offenders are frequently arrested for nonpayment and then get fired from their jobs. This lack of common sense pushes the door wide open. The second is the attitude of parole/probation officers. They see jail as the only means of public protection.

The bigger issue that actually keeps the jail door spinning at high speed is the citizens' need for vengeance. By refusing any form of redemption we place ourselves at risk by creating the bitter climate of rejection that fosters crime. It is 42 years late, but let's help offenders get work, slow the revolving door, restore our own dignity, and take a huge bite out of human misery.

Bob Ferguson
VANCOUVER

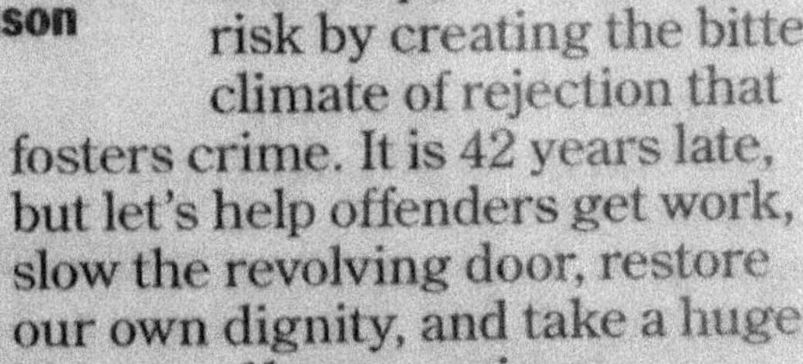

www.ingramcontent.com/pod-product-compliance
Lightning Source LLC
Chambersburg PA
CBHW081248250726

48654CB00012B/1528